# DENES AGAY'S LEARNING TO

# EASY CLASSICAL

**Wise Publications**
part of The Music Sales Group
London / New York / Paris / Sydney / Copenhagen / Berlin / Madrid / Tokyo

Published by
**Wise Publications**
14-15 Berners Street, London W1T 3LJ, UK

Exclusive Distributors:
**Music Sales Limited**
Distribution Centre, Newmarket Road,
Bury St Edmunds, Suffolk IP33 3YB, UK
**Music Sales Pty Limited**
20 Resolution Drive,
Caringbah, NSW 2229, Australia

Order No. AM1003981
ISBN 978-1-78038-279-1

Edited by Ruth Searle
Illustrated by Jon Burgerman
Designed by Lizzie Barrand

Printed in the EU

www.musicsales.com

# ODE TO JOY
## (FROM SYMPHONY NO. 9, FOURTH MOVEMENT)
### LUDWIG VAN BEETHOVEN

Allegro assai

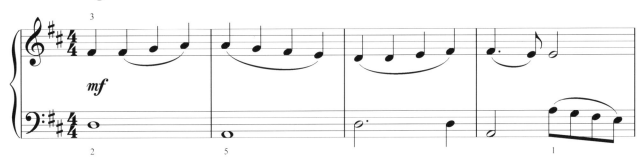

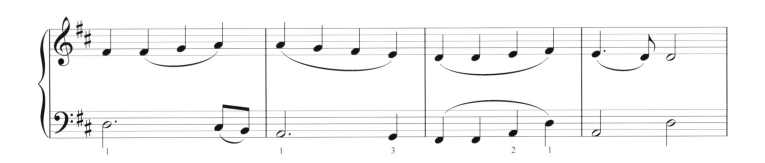

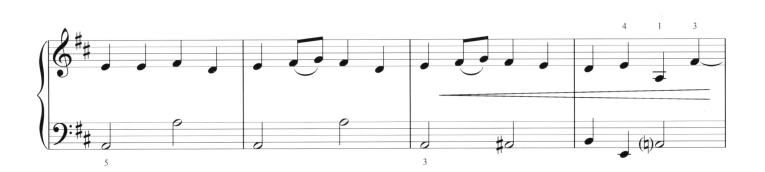

# MOONLIGHT SONATA
## LUDWIG VAN BEETHOVEN

**Adagio sostenuto**

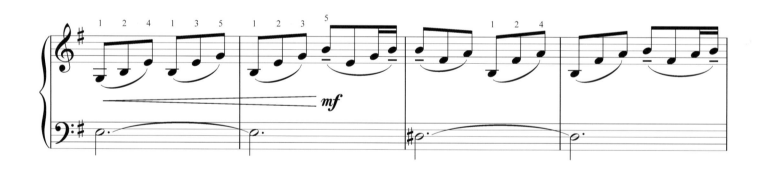

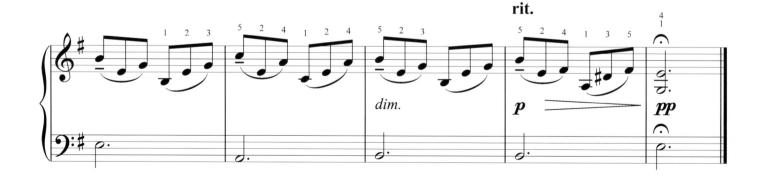

# GREENSLEEVES
## TRADITIONAL

**Briskly, in 1**

# WILLIAM TELL OVERTURE
## (FINALE)
## GIOACCHINO ROSSINI

**Allegro vivace**

*D.C. al Fine*
*(with repeat)*

# SARABANDE IN D MINOR

## GEORGE FRIDERIC HANDEL

Adagio

# THEME FROM SWAN LAKE

## PYOTR ILYICH TCHAIKOVSKY

**Moderato espressivo**

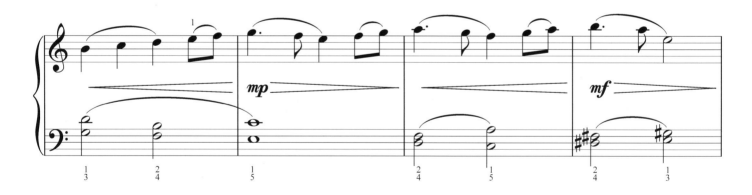

# FÜR ELISE
## LUDWIG VAN BEETHOVEN

Poco moto

# THE CAN CAN
## JACQUES OFFENBACH

**Allegretto moderato**

# LARGO (FROM 'FROM THE NEW WORLD')

## ANTONÍN DVOŘÁK

Largo

# MINUET IN G
## JOHANN SEBASTIAN BACH

**Allegretto**

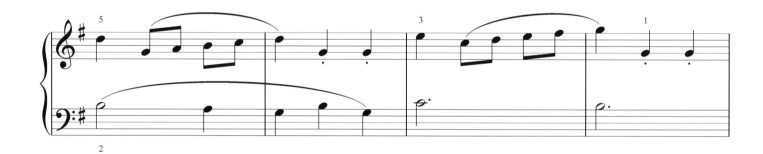

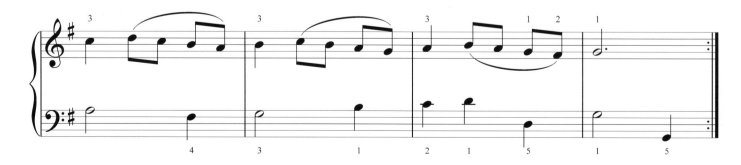

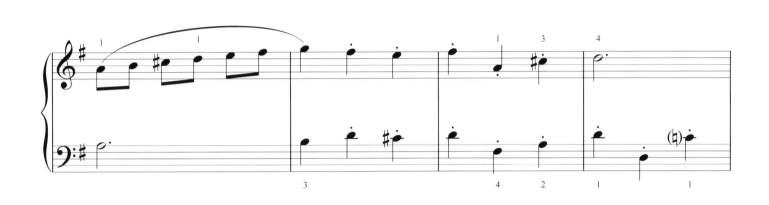

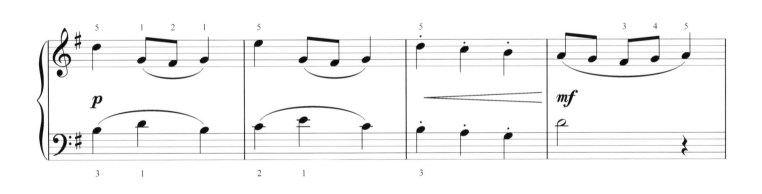

# PAVANE
## GABRIEL FAURÉ

**Andante molto moderato**

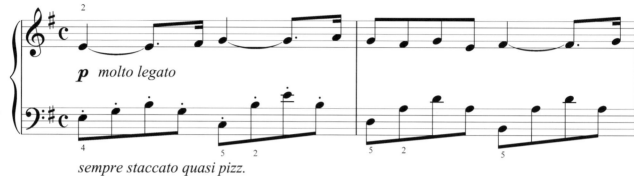

*p* *molto legato*

*sempre staccato quasi pizz.*

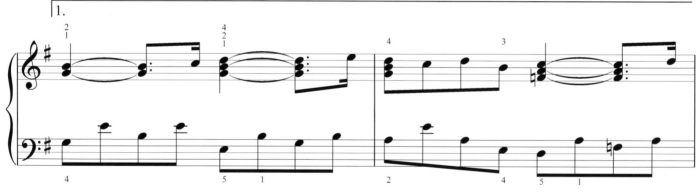

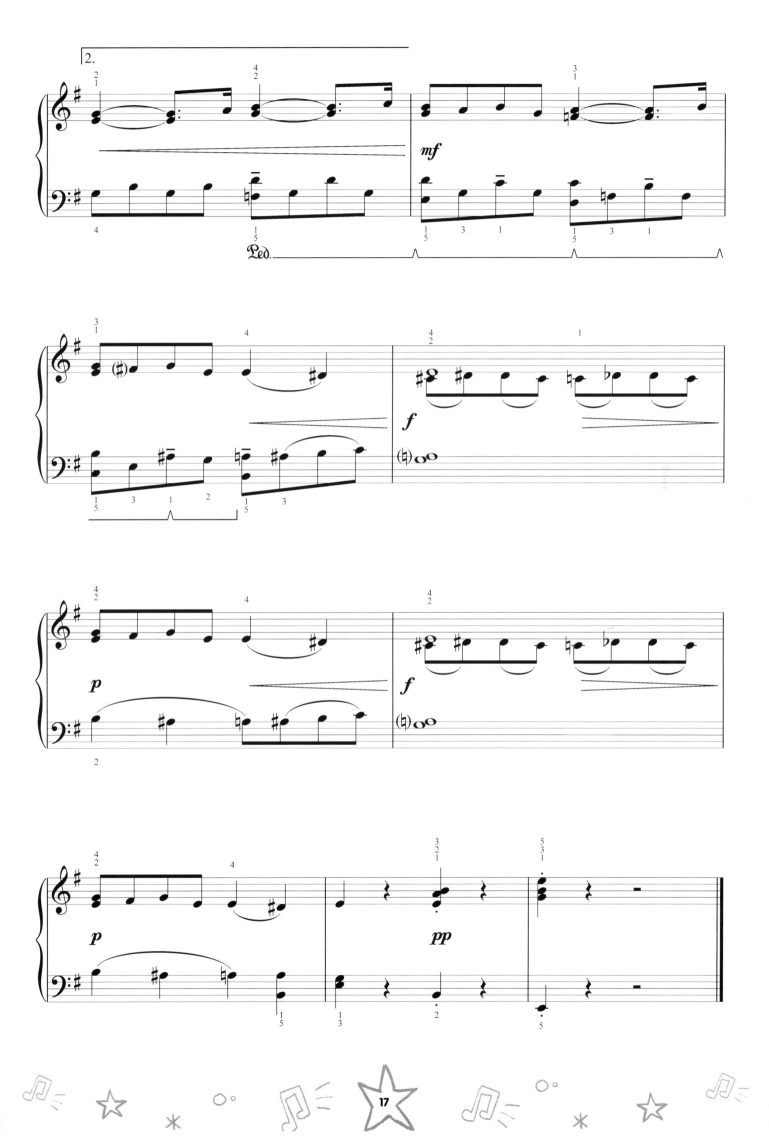

# PRELUDE NO.1 IN C
## JOHANN SEBASTIAN BACH

**Allegretto**

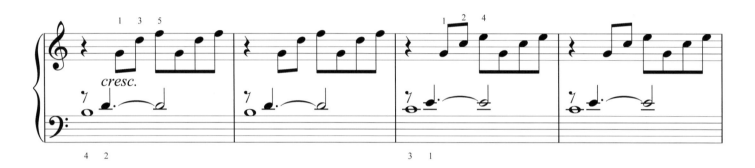

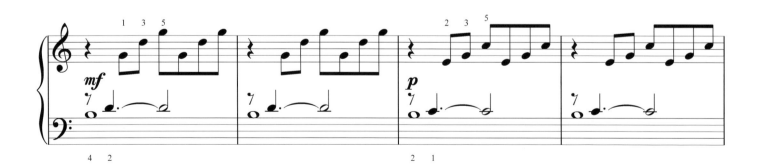

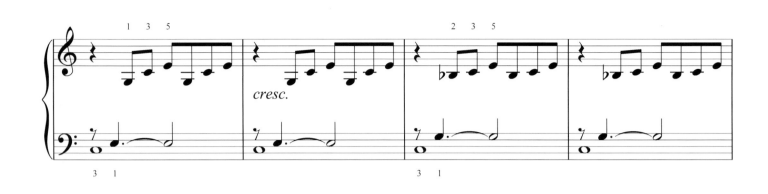

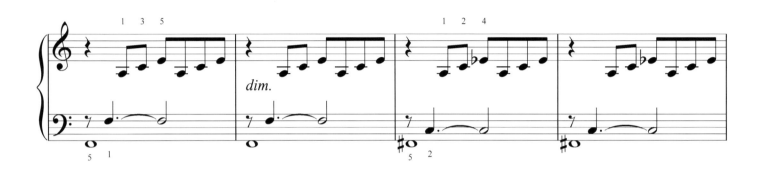

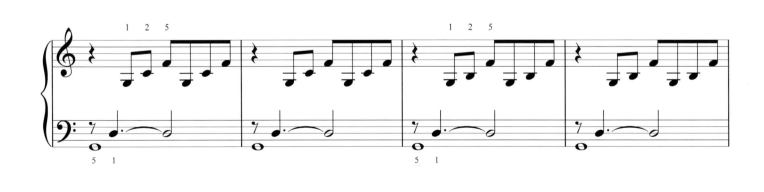

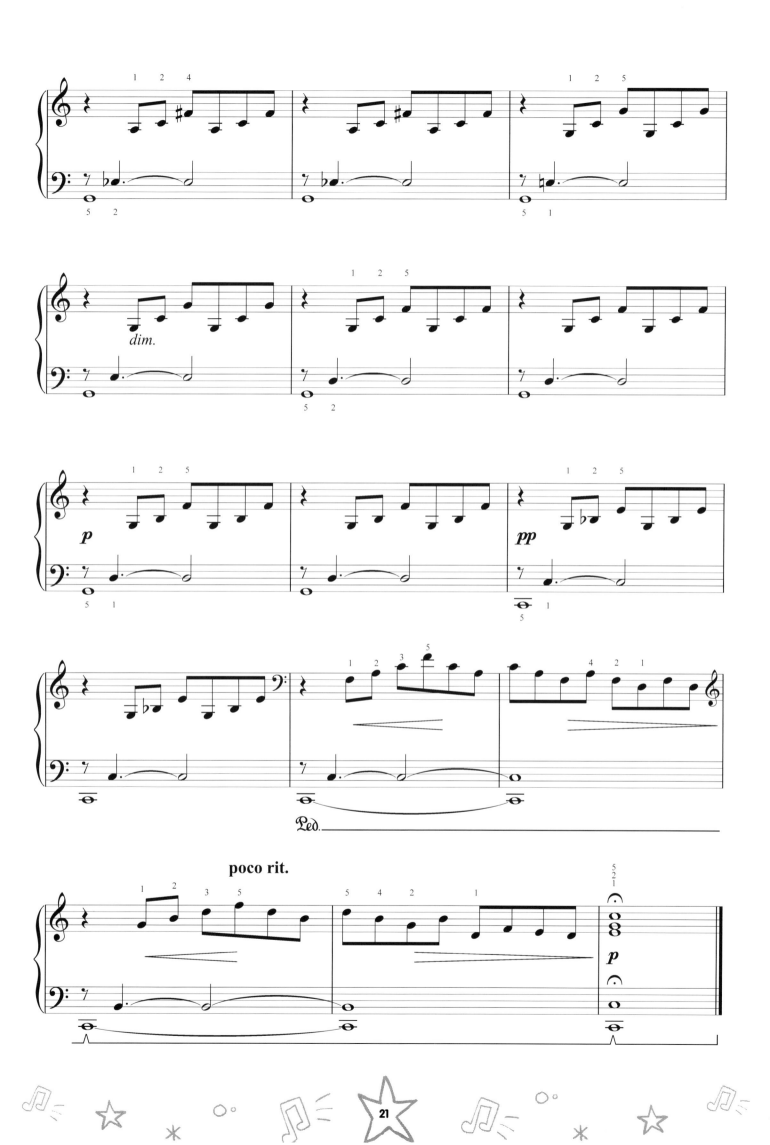

# JUPITER (FROM 'THE PLANETS' OP. 32)
## GUSTAV HOLST

**Andante maestoso**

sempre cresc.

ff

allargando

# CANON IN D
## JOHANN PACHELBEL

**Sostenuto**

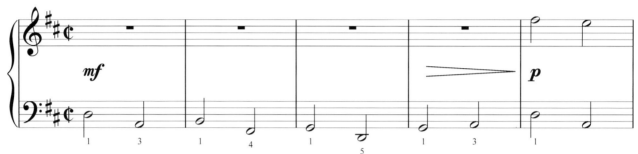

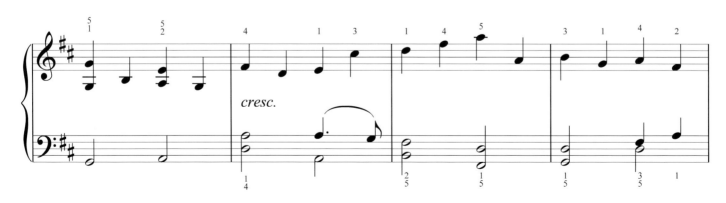

# MORNING MOOD
## (FROM 'PEER GYNT')
### EDVARD GRIEG

**Largo**

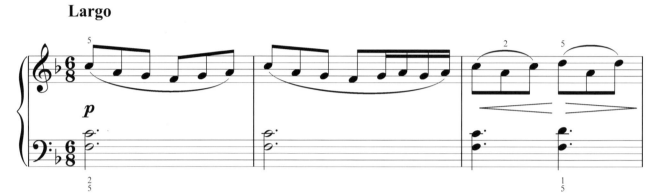

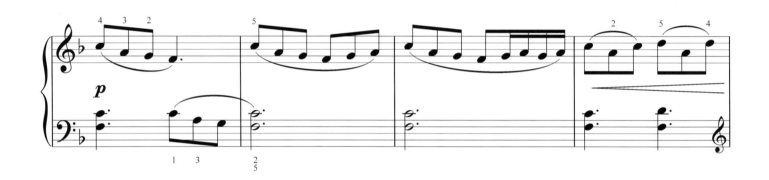

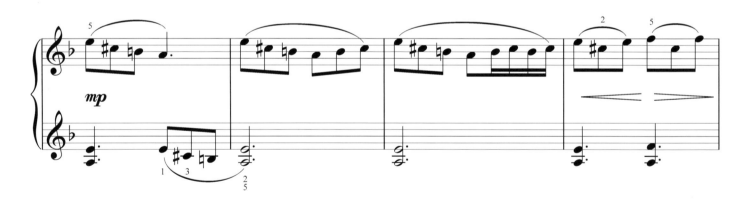

# SPRING
## (FROM 'THE FOUR SEASONS')
### ANTONIO VIVALDI

**Allegro**

# THE SORCERER'S APPRENTICE
## PAUL DUKAS

# EINE KLEINE NACHTMUSIK

## WOLFGANG AMADEUS MOZART

Allegro